THE SPIRIT OF THE LETTER
IN PAINTING

THE SPIRIT OF THE LETTER
IN PAINTING

TEXT BY JEAN LEYMARIE

Translated from the French by James Emmons

PUBLISHED BY HALLMARK CARDS - AN ALBERT SKIRA CREATION

On the title page:

Rembrandt van Rijn (1606-1669). Jan Six writing in his Country House at Ijmond, about 1655-1656. Pen and bistre wash. (5 ¼ × 8 ¾″) Louvre, Paris.

★

Contents

List of Colorplates

Where are the homes of yesterday and the quiet seclusion of long afternoons, as the town clock tolled the hours, or of evenings by candlelight, when one had the leisure and the inclination to set pen to paper and write long letters? One cannot help feeling a certain nostalgia in turning over the pages of this book with its sequence of great paintings from Rembrandt to Renoir, by way of Vermeer, Chardin and Corot, which not only reflect the spirit of the letter in painting but evoke a whole way of life that has passed away forever. What the reader will find in the following pages is nothing less than a pictorial essay on the social graces of a certain age, which reached its height in Europe from the seventeenth to the nineteenth century, first in Holland, then in Paris, London, Venice and the Germany of the Romantic period.

When he founded Hallmark Cards over fifty years ago, Mr. Joyce Hall realized that greeting cards which elevate sentiment and foster human relations are in many ways the twentieth century counterpart of the personal letters immortalized in the painting and writing of earlier times. Like the letters of past centuries, greeting cards in our time commemorate the memorable occasions of life and draw closer the ties that bind us to family and friends.

It was my wife who conceived the idea of this book. Would it not be interesting, she suggested, to show how strong and pervasive a theme letter writing and letter reading have been in the painting of the last three centuries when social letter writing was at its height? Mr. Hall responded enthusiastically and so did Professor Jean Leymarie, who has written a text in which social history and art appreciation are expertly combined. I am happy to see the book published under the auspices of Hallmark Cards.

Albert Skira

Jean-Baptiste-Siméon Chardin (1699-1779). Boy spinning a Top (detail), about 1738. Louvre, Paris.

Introduction

This book is the outcome of an idea which was not my own, but which I confess to have found most attractive and stimulating: to bring together some thirty masterpieces of painting, ranging from the seventeenth to the twentieth century, in which a letter is the keynote of the composition. The reader will soon discover that this is not just an anthology of pictures on a particularly charming theme. The carefully selected illustrations go to form an organic whole, and together they show, in the most vivid colors, the spirit in which the great painters from Rembrandt to Renoir have treated the subject of letters and letter writing.

Men have been writing each other letters for at least five thousand years. The early civilizations of Egypt, Mesopotamia and China, together with Greek and Latin antiquity, have left us many examples of both private and official correspondence. Each of these vast cultures, with its corps of professional literati personified by the Scribe and the Mandarin, invented its own mode of writing and also its own writing material: papyrus in the Nile Valley, clay tablets in Mesopotamia, and silk in China where the same brush was used for writing and painting, and where the calligraphy of a letter was no less important than its contents. The Greeks and Romans used wax tablets on which the letter was scratched with a stylus; after being read, it could be obliterated by smoothing the wax and replaced by the reply. We actually have a few letters written by the Greek philosopher Epicurus, and a great many by the Roman writers Cicero, Seneca and Pliny. Several ancient sculptures in low relief illustrate the dispatch and delivery of mail by mounted couriers, showing post horses at relay stations on the main roads and revealing the existence of a well organized postal system.

From about the third century B.C. to the beginning of the Christian era, tablets and papyrus were gradually superseded by parchment, a more convenient and durable substance which remained the standard writing material until the end of the Middle Ages and even beyond. Parchment and a whiter, finer grained variety of it, vellum, proved to be an ideal support for book illumination, one of the major art forms of the Middle Ages.

The Epistles of the New Testament (of which the most famous are those written by St. Paul) and the epistolary writings of the Fathers of the Church gave rise to an immense body of exegetical and apologetical literature, very often in the form of letters, which filled the vast libraries of the medieval monasteries. Grandiose images of the Prophets, Evangelists, Apostles and Doctors of the Church, shown pen in hand, writing in the throes of divine inspiration, remained for centuries, from early medieval manuscript illuminations to the Sistine Chapel and Rembrandt, one of the major themes of religious painting.

Except for government couriers, the only reliable and regular postal services of the Middle Ages were those operated by the universities and the monastic orders. Miniatures and tapestries, for example the famous

Bayeux Tapestry, often represent royal and princely messengers hastening on their errands, either on foot or on horseback. Except for those of a few powerful noblemen and church dignitaries, who had dispatch riders in their employ, private letters were rare and had to be entrusted to the care of passing travelers, itinerant merchants and pilgrims. Marco Polo, in the late thirteenth century, describes the elaborate network of relay stations maintained by the Great Khan on the roads of China for the speedy dispatch of messages and letters.

As the Middle Ages drew to a close, scenes of everyday life and particularly of feminine life became a frequent subject in the last illuminated manuscripts, which were painted in the courtly style of International Gothic art. Many of these miniature paintings illustrate the works of Boccaccio, Christine de Pisan and above all the *Heroides* of Ovid. Sometimes they show fine ladies, or fine gentlemen, in the fashionable dress of the period, penning their love letters in the privacy of boudoir or study. The same theme, with the same atmosphere of leisure and refinement, appears in Persian and Islamic miniature painting.

Paper, invented in China at some time in the remote past and transmitted to Europe by the Arabs, came into general use in the fifteenth century. Being cheaply produced and easily handled, it soon supplanted all other writing materials. The introduction of paper coincided with the decline of book illumination, the rise of easel painting, and the invention of printing. The growing output of printed matter brought the Renaissance to a climax, speeded up the Reformation, and stimulated the revival of secular learning by diffusing the literature of Antiquity and the writings of the Humanists.

The early sixteenth century saw the publication of some of the finest books ever printed, and also marked one of the great ages of portrait painting, in two distinct styles: monumental and imposing in Italy, realistic and intimate in Northern Europe. Painters continued to portray the great religious writers venerated throughout the Middle Ages, particularly St. Jerome, patron saint of the Humanists, showing him in the dress and setting of their own time (as in the pictures by Carpaccio and Dürer). But they also painted portraits of contemporary scholars and men of letters, shown surrounded by their books and writing paraphernalia, shown sometimes too with one of the many letters they exchanged with correspondents all over Europe in Latin, the universal language of that day. The most famous of these scholars was Erasmus of Rotterdam, who sat in turn to three of the greatest artists of Northern Europe, each of whom was a master of portraiture: Quentin Massys, Hans Holbein, and Dürer.

Fine though they are, we have not included illustrations of any of these humanist portraits because the letters occasionally figuring in them are no more than symbols or accessories, without any real connection with the mood or psychology of the sitter. Only Erasmus is shown genuinely absorbed in the page he is writing—but he is not shown as a letter writer. Moreover, the correspondence of the sixteenth century that has come down to us is, for the most part, scholarly or dogmatic in nature. When private affairs are occasionally touched on, even between near relations, they are restricted to practical household matters, with little expression of personal feelings. The rare outbursts of self-expression in letters of the period maintain a certain reserve and formality, only natural in an age of partisan violence, when to speak one's mind was to risk one's life.

We have also refrained from illustrating famous portraits by Titian, Velazquez and Rembrandt in which the figure merely stands or sits with a sheet of paper in his hand (presumably in some cases a letter) instead of the traditional accessory of a book, a fan, or gloves. The gray tint of the paper contrasts with the black of the costume and creates delicate pictorial effects particularly sought after by the Spanish masters, from El Greco to Goya; but this accessory has no bearing on the model's inner life. On the other hand, among the strange Netherlandish Mannerists who were followers of Quentin Massys and catered for the luxury-loving, cosmopolitan clientele of Antwerp, the singular works of an unidentified painter known as the Master of the Female Half-Lengths call for special mention here. His stylishly dressed young women, shown singly or in groups, making music or reading and writing letters, foreshadow those of Terborch, but with a certain shallowness, affectation and frivolous display of luxury articles (in the guise of religious attributes) that have no place among the works, all in an intimate and contemplative vein, to which we have confined ourselves here.

It was in France in the seventeenth century that the art of letter writing, in many ways a by-product of the elegant and polished school of literature associated with the drawing-room circles sponsored by society women, came to be practiced for its own sake and it soon enjoyed a great vogue throughout Europe. But for any trace of all this in painting, now given over to the theatrical turbulence of Baroque and the solemn pomps of Classicism, we look in vain—except in the genre painting of Holland, with its intimate glimpses of home life. This type of painting took its rise in the mid-seventeenth century, beginning with Rembrandt. The theme of a letter being read, written or received, in the tranquil seclusion of the home, where woman ruled supreme, together with the plays of light and psychological insights that arise from letter reading or letter writing, and the disappointments and revelations incidental to the letter's contents—this was a favorite theme with Vermeer, Terborch, Metsu and Pieter de Hooch.

The Dutch masters exerted a strong influence on all European painting in the eighteenth century, when the same subject was treated even more often and in a greater variety of ways. Society life and drawing-room conversation centered on woman, and this was the century *par excellence* of wit and repartee, of intrigues and flirtations, of new ideas and libertarian theories, all of which, when the party was over or the "season" ended, offered fascinating pretexts for lengthy letters. For the eighteenth century was the heyday of letter writing, not only as a literary device in the novelist's hands, but as a fine art in its own right, complete with its own paraphernalia, accessories, furniture, and methods of dispatch. Thus it provided a theme of never-ending interest for painters: Chardin, Boucher and Fragonard in France, Liotard in Switzerland, Longhi in Venice, and Gainsborough in England.

By the nineteenth century letter writing had become less of an art and more of a personal affair, quite distinct from literature. The modern postal system had everywhere come into operation much as we know it today. The theme of the letter in painting was taken over chiefly by illustrators and little masters, like Achille Devéria in France and Moritz von Schwind in Germany. But it was also given masterly interpretations by such great painters as Goya, David, Corot, Manet and Renoir. The latter, though working as always on his own original and delightful lines, recaptures something of the spirit of both Vermeer and Fragonard. And with Renoir our cycle of letter pictures is brought to a close. Several fine still lifes in which letters play a leading part add a spice of variety to the sequence of figure paintings.

It will be noticed, and may cause surprise, that some very famous masterpieces are not included here: Rembrandt's *Bathsheba*, holding the royal message on which her fate depends; David's *Marat*, stabbed to death in his bath, with the fatal letter of Charlotte Corday still in his hand; and the still life painted by Van Gogh after his release from hospital, which contains a letter from his brother Theo, his last-remaining link with society and the world at large. These works do not fall within the scope of this book. Their dramatic tension would have disrupted the unity of a picture sequence whose harmony is compounded, above all, of intimacy and communicative charm. Indeed it is symptomatic—and we would emphasize the extraordinary chance of thus seeing them grouped together around the same theme—that the keynotes, for each of the three centuries spanned by this volume, are struck by Vermeer, Chardin and Corot, who share not only a common mood of pensive contemplation, but an unsurpassable mastery of the painter's craft.

Today, when rather than pen a letter so many of us type it, or else resort to the telephone (or even the tape recorder), one cannot help feeling a certain nostalgia, even a pang of regret, as one contemplates these quiet pictures of a not very distant past, when there still was leisure for letter writing, and still taste enough to phrase a letter gracefully, to have it sent with a bouquet of flowers and smilingly perused by a fair lady who could appreciate the spirit of it. "All her warmth was of the spirit," said her cousin Bussy de Rabutin of Madame de Sévigné, thus justifying the title of this book and letting us into the secret of perhaps the finest letter writer of all time.

The main text of this book is set in 14 point Garamond italic type, whose graceful design, akin to handwriting, seemed particularly well suited to the theme and spirit of the works illustrated.

1

This opening chapter deals exclusively with Dutch painting, the first and indeed the only school in the seventeenth century to adopt the theme of the letter, as we have defined it, to develop it as an aspect of daily life in the home, and to establish it as a full-fledged type of genre painting illustrated by a large, homogeneous body of works of outstanding quality.

The small Dutch Republic was at the height of its power and prosperity in the middle of the seventeenth century. After her long, heroic struggle for freedom and independence, Holland now held her own successfully against powerful neighbors, ruled the seas and founded a colonial empire (in Rembrandt's time New York was still "New Amsterdam"). Holland took the lead in commerce and banking, and with her democratic, middle-class society based on Erasmian liberalism, she set an example to the rest of Europe. Preceding France and England, she was the first great modern nation. She welcomed Descartes within her borders, gave birth to Spinoza, and founded international law. Cultural and social standards were higher there than elsewhere, and education was more widespread. Her universities, scholars, and humanists were famous, but it was in her painters that Holland found supreme fulfillment. Rejecting historical, religious and mythological subjects, and with them Baroque pomposity and classical idealism, the Dutch masters originated an art essentially realistic and homely, intended for the average man and the private home, and strongly conditioned by the national life of Holland, although inseparable from the European context; and the most characteristic form of this art is genre painting.

"The Dutch school," wrote Fromentin, "centers on what is known as genre." Genre painting is the representation of everyday life and its familiar surroundings, authentic and unidealized. Reflecting the manners and fashions, the costumes and customs of the day, and emphasizing differences of class, age, sex and occupation, genre painting changed with each successive generation and took on a local color according to its place of origin. The brief Golden Age of Dutch painting spans no more than three generations, represented in turn by Frans Hals at Haarlem, Rembrandt at Amsterdam, and Vermeer at Delft.

The first phase was one of buoyant, not to say braggart optimism, the second one of high moral purpose and soul-searchings, and the third a serene reflection of material well-being and social refinement. Haarlem and Amsterdam were the centers of a genuinely national art. Delft was a provincial backwater into which filtered two distinct currents of influence: the Caravaggesque tradition transmitted by way of Utrecht, the Dutch city in closest touch with Italy, and the indigenous tradition elaborated at Leyden, the university city where Rembrandt formed his style. Like Shakespeare, Rembrandt transcends all categories and limitations. His "Bathsheba" (1654, Louvre), represented at her toilette with King David's letter in her hand, is the most moving nude in all painting. This Biblical theme soon gave rise to many imitations. It was taken over by Jan Steen who, in a picture of about 1655-1660 (formerly in the Nicolas Collection, Paris), transposed it with his usual gusto into a profane and elegant genre scene in the manner of Terborch. While the worldly minded intimist painters

Jan Vermeer (1632-1675). Young Woman reading a Letter (detail), about 1658. Gemäldegalerie, Dresden.

(with whom we shall largely be dealing here) took little interest in drawing for its own sake, Rembrandt, on the contrary, left a vast body of drawings and etchings, and it is in these works above all that, with unexampled power and truthfulness, he recorded the many-sided aspects of Dutch scenery and daily life. An admirable pen-and-ink drawing with a bistre wash (reproduced on the title page) probably represents Rembrandt's patrician friend Jan Six, about the time when they saw most of each other (1655-1656), shown writing a letter in his country house at Ijmond. The window opens on a landscape that is almost Chinese in its breadth and concision; a boat beyond the wooden dike and a church tower on the opposite bank punctuate the broad expanse of the river as it flows into the Zuyder Zee.

In the period with which we are now concerned, the two opposing trends of Dutch genre painting were represented by Jan Steen (1626-1679) and Gerard Terborch (1617-1681), contemporaries of Vermeer (1632-1675) and indeed his elders, though both survived him. One trend, exuberant and popular, was localized chiefly in Haarlem, where it was maintained by Adriaen van Ostade (1610-1684); the other, more intimate and delicate in execution, took its rise in Leyden with Gerard Dou (1613-1675). Curiously enough, the quiet theme of letter writing was occasionally treated by Steen, and even by Van Ostade who specialized in uproarious scenes of low life; yet not a single letter writer appears to figure among the host of students, scholars and men of letters represented by Gerard Dou, who probably painted more books than any other artist before or since.

The early generation of genre painters, truculent and combative, schooled by Frans Hals, instinctively fixed its eyes on such permanent types of humanity, little affected by education or the fashions of the day, as soldiers, peasants and young people, and showed them satisfying the basic instincts of healthy manhood in drinking bouts, games and love-making, or indulging in noisy revelry in taverns and guard rooms, at village fairs and weddings. But gradually, as business prospered and better times came in, Dutch society settled down to a sedater, more refined way of living, and the scene shifted toward home life, from which roisterers were excluded and in which placid housewives watched over the family's well-being, servants worked hard, and pious grandmothers set the tone—that atmosphere of blameless domesticity, studious composure and prevailing sentimentalism so well conveyed by some of Rembrandt's pupils, such as Nicolaes Maes (1634-1693) and Gerard Dou. Finally, under the influence of Terborch, the middle-class domestic picture gave place to scenes of high society, of well-dressed people with ample means and leisure for their elegant pastimes; to conversation pieces and so-called satin gown pictures. These were refined to a crystalline perfection at Delft by the genius of Vermeer, while in Amsterdam they were given a pretentious, ornate form which revealed foreign influences and by the same token pointed toward the decadence of the school.

In France, in the seventeenth century, the customs and usages of polite society gained in refinement, chiefly under feminine influence, in the drawing rooms of the so-called Précieux ("mannered"), with whom the art of letter writing, derived from conversation, became for the first time a distinct literary form. Its initiator in France was Guez de Balzac (1597-1654), who had lived in Holland in his youth, and whose twenty-seven volumes of letters, published in his lifetime, enjoyed a tremendous success. At the famous Hôtel de Rambouillet the best society of Paris forgathered; its equivalent in Holland was Muiden Castle near Amsterdam, residence of the Dutch poet and historian Pieter Cornelissen Hooft. Here, until his death in 1647, Hooft kept open house to all the celebrities of Holland—the poet Joost

Gabriel Metsu (1629-1667). Man writing a Letter. (11 × 10⅛″)
Musée Fabre, Montpellier.

Gerard Terborch (1617-1681). Woman writing a Letter, about 1654. (15⅜ × 11⅜″)
Stichting Johan Maurits van Nassau, Mauritshuis, The Hague.

van den Vondel, Constantin Huygens, the Visscher sisters, the singer Francisca Duarte. In the Muiden circle music was made, poetry recited and extemporized, games played, and letters written in an atmosphere of genial humanism largely inspired by Montaigne and Erasmus. Hooft's own letters have been described as "the most charming ever published in the Dutch language."

Handwriting, taught calligraphically, formed the basis of education in Holland, and girls above all were given a solid grounding in the practice of letter writing, now increasingly widespread in a country where the needs of war and commerce kept men traveling and corresponding. The postal system, controlled by the municipalities, soon became the best organized in the world and thousands of Dutch ships plying the seven seas were already carrying mail in special watertight pouches. Letters were as a rule sealed with sticks of sealing wax. Messages of a tender nature accompanied by flowers effectively overcame the constraints of Calvinism and the hesitant speech of a people whose finest faculties were visual. Letter-writing manuals of all kinds were already in existence in the seventeenth century, covering business correspondence, invitations, letters of condolence—and of course love letters. In difficult cases or on solemn occasions recourse was had to public letter writers versed in the lore of popular proverbs, and with a scholarly store of emblematic maxims at the tip of their pen. Even the humblest home was provided with a writing desk, with goose quills or reed pens, with a few treasured volumes and a stock of fine paper manufactured by the mills of Guelders or Zaandam.

The cultural climate of the age, as outlined above, accounts for the appearance of the letter in the thematic repertory of Dutch genre painting, at a time when French influence was molding the style of upper-class social life in Holland. The heyday of this theme lies within a well-defined period of time: from the Peace of Westphalia in 1648, when the Elzevir Press in Leyden published a selection of Guez de Balzac's "Letters," to the Peace of Nimeguen in 1678, the year which saw the publication in Paris of Madame de Lafayette's "La Princesse de Clèves," the first consummate example of the modern psychological novel, as fresh and readable today as it was then. In 1669, the hypothetical date of Vermeer's "Love Letter," appeared the famous "Letters of a Portuguese Nun," one of the great revelations of a woman's heart. In that same year Madame de Sévigné married her daughter to the Comte de Grignan and began with her that voluminous and incomparable correspondence which Marcel Proust, fittingly enough, admired as devoutly as he did the painting of Vermeer.

Although it had occasionally been treated before, in a very different spirit, as in the small pictures by Dirck Hals (1591-1656) at Mainz (1631) and Philadelphia, the real creator of the letter theme in painting was Gerard Terborch. Born in 1617 at Zwolle in the north Dutch province of Overyssel, son of a cultivated patrician who was himself an amateur artist, he learned to paint while still a boy and completed his training in Amsterdam and Haarlem. From 1635 to 1645 he roamed through England, France, Italy and Spain, enriching his experience both as a painter and a man of the world, without compromising his own originality. "Though he mixed with kings, princes, ambassadors, cardinals, and the great of many lands," wrote Thoré-Bürger, who just a hundred years ago rescued both Terborch and Vermeer from oblivion, "he never lost his naturalness, while gaining from these contacts that rare distinction and exquisite grace which make him an ideal interpreter of the Dutch upper class of the period. None of the foreign masters left any mark on him, though in some mysterious way he absorbed all that was best in them. If he owes something to any one of them, it is perhaps to Velazquez, whose silvery greens, with their elusive, softly blended nuances, appear in some of his pictures."

An accomplished portraitist and genre painter, Terborch is the finest exponent of Dutch intimism. No window is visible in any of his works; closed to the outside world, they deal exclusively with the intimate, leisured refinements of Dutch home life. Conception, treatment, color and discreetly limited dimensions combine to produce a perfect picture. His constant practice of portrait painting sharpened his naturally observant eye and developed the keen psychological insight that went into his genre scenes. Woman is the hub of that world and she has nothing else to do than reading, writing letters, looking pretty, making music; a not unwilling captive of the daily round, she can give herself up to daydreams, while seemingly busy with her simple household tasks.

In 1654 Terborch retired to Deventer, in his native province, where he lived until his death in 1681. There he painted perhaps the finest of his conversation pieces and "tableaux de mode," or "satin gown" pictures, as they are called because of the emphasis on rich apparel. When Frans van Mieris and Gabriel Metsu portray the new-rich burghers of Holland, we are conscious that the sitters feel ill at ease in their fine new clothes. But Terborch's figures in their velvets, silks and satin seem to the manner born; it is hard to imagine them dressed otherwise. Not only does fashionable dress indicate the model's social status and display the artist's technical skill; here it expresses the innate distinction of a style and a way of life. The great German critic Heinrich Wölfflin distinguishes Terborch from his rival Metsu solely by his rendering of the folds in satin gowns—"no better drawn, but more deeply felt."

Gerard Terborch (1617-1681). Woman reading a Letter, 1662. C. von Pannwitz Collection.

At least fifteen of Terborch's finest genre pieces, ranging in date from 1650 to 1670, are letter pictures: a letter being read, written or sealed in a bourgeois boudoir or drawing room, sometimes within range of prying eyes, or dictated by an officer camping in the field, delivered by village postman or private messenger, and arousing in the recipient expectant pleasure, pained surprise or bitter disappointment solaced by a glass of wine.

From this varied cycle of letter pictures, which from several points of view would justify a detailed analysis, we have selected two examples, the most secretive and meditative of them all. Suggested, possibly, by the illustrations in books of emblems, Terborch's "Woman writing a Letter" (about 1654, Mauritshuis, The Hague) is the prototype of this new theme (hitherto there had been women reading, but never writing), which from now on was to inspire Vermeer, Metsu, Mieris, Carel de Moor, and many others. The table and inkstand, the Oriental carpet and the canopied bed in the background, had already figured in other pictures by Terborch, and so had the same young woman with décolleté and blond ringlets. In the soft penumbra of the room, with its elusive gradations of tone from scarlet to green, and the exquisite note struck by the pearl eardrop and the blue ribbon, the light glows on her thoughtful forehead and pretty shoulders, as she drives her goose quill over the letter paper.

"Observe how daintily and cautiously she goes about it," writes Frans Hellens in a charming description of this picture. "She is not one to commit her thoughts to paper at random. Unfaltering, if perhaps a trifle heavy, the hand behind the pen records her thoughts, moving briskly straight to the point. Just now, when she paused to read over her letter, all the light fell full on her face. But no sooner does she start writing than a mysterious flux of light links up the speaking hand with the forehead that seems to be the source of all

the ripples of emotion traversing her face. And how clearly does the curve of that forehead stand out against the shadows of the alcove. It reflects the ebb and flow of thought, spontaneous yet discreetly held in check. We can tell from her expression the subtle pleasure she takes in writing. From the quivering of the nostrils we can guess that a clever idea has just occurred to her, while the firm line of the lips shows she has decided exactly what form to give it. In her self-absorption she scarcely bends over the table." Terborch suggests without insisting, always leaving scope for mystery or ambiguity.

In the "Woman reading a Letter" (C. von Pannwitz Collection), a picture remarkable for the same subtle focus of light and attention on face and hands, we recognize Gesina, the artist's sister, who often posed for him. Here she is dressed in black, in mourning for her father who died in May 1662—which thus enables us to date the picture accurately. Her auburn hair is draped in a black silk veil, but her arm is bare to the elbow. Gleaming on the gilt ewer and candlestick, sunlight kindles deep-toned harmonies of red and gray-green. Terborch's masterpiece, "The Letter" (Buckingham Palace, London), is a skillful combination of these two motifs around a single table, with a seated woman writing and a standing woman reading, beneath the richly wrought chandelier that lights up so many comfortably furnished Dutch and Flemish interiors from Van Eyck to Vermeer.

Terborch's influence on the course of Dutch genre painting was very marked. His best pupil, Caspar Netscher (1639-1684), court portraitist at The Hague, modeled his scenes of domestic life and his pictures of letter writers (Gemäldegalerie, Dresden) on those of his master, though he came increasingly under the influence of French art and French fashions. This was also the case with Jan Verkolje (1650-1693), whose "Message" (1674, Mauritshuis, The Hague) is one of his most successful works. Totally absent

Jan Vermeer (1632-1675). Lady writing a Letter (detail), about 1670. Sir Alfred Beit Collection, London.

in the work of Gerard Dou, the theme of the letter appears frequently in that of his leading disciples, Gabriel Metsu (1629-1667) and Frans van Mieris (1635-1681). Metsu settled in Amsterdam in 1657 and, without abandoning the minute precision characteristic of the Leyden school, assimilated the joint influences of Rembrandt, Terborch and Vermeer. His famous companion pieces in the Beit Collection, London, the "Man writing

Jan Vermeer (1632-1675). Girl in Blue reading a Letter (detail), about 1665. Rijksmuseum, Amsterdam.

a Letter" and "Lady reading a Letter," have often been compared with Vermeer (in particular with Vermeer's "Lady writing a Letter" in the same collection), and the beauty of their colors and the solidity of their construction justify the comparison. The massive figures stand out against light-colored walls, the man in deep black, the lady in delicate pink and yellow beside a maidservant in brown and blue.

"The painterly qualities of these pictures are worthy of Vermeer," writes A.B. de Vries of the two Metsus in the Beit Collection, "and only a difference of a spiritual order separates the two artists." But this spiritual difference is all-important; it marks the gulf between mere story-telling and pure poetry. Even as a story-teller, Metsu has neither the tact of Terborch nor the gusto of Jan Steen, often masking the shallowness of his psychology under a trivial show of animation. His virtues are those of an executant, those above all of a fine colorist, expert in playing off warm harmonies of red and yellow against blacks and grays. We see Metsu at his most intimate and rewarding in the small panel illustrated here, "Man writing a Letter," one of the little known gems of the Valedau Bequest, a superlative collection of Dutch and Flemish little masters donated in its entirety to the Musée Fabre at Montpellier. The letter writer has paused with his pen in the air to reread what he has just written, and judge of its effect, while a serving woman approaches with a lighted candle. A full-bodied Rembrandtesque chiaroscuro absorbing forms and even swallowing up the red Oriental carpet—a motif often given undue prominence in genre pictures of the time—plunges the whole scene in an atmosphere of mystery and subdued emotion. "Letter Writing" by Frans van Mieris (1680, Rijksmuseum, Amsterdam) presents a similar layout, reversed and absolutely symmetrical, but in a scintillating miniaturist style much closer in spirit to that of Gerard Dou.

"Vermeer," writes André Malraux, "is only another Dutch intimist or genre painter for a sociologist, but not for an artist." Admittedly genre painting, in his hands, attains to a crystalline perfection which transmutes the anecdote, the ostensible subject matter, into pure contemplation—or, if you like, into pure painting. The fact remains that his pictures are full of symbolic allusions whose meaning still baffles and eludes us, ignorant as we are of the

practices and habits of thought of the time. Out of the twenty-six interiors legitimately attributed to Vermeer, seven go to form a set of variations on the theme of the letter, coupled in several cases with musical instruments.

After several "trial pictures" in various moods, Biblical, mythological or Caravaggesque, Vermeer achieved a style of his own in the "Young Woman reading a Letter" (Gemäldegalerie, Dresden). Shown in profile against a light-colored wall, motionless, engrossed in what she is reading, the young woman—a figure inspired by Terborch—reveals herself to us only in the reflection of her face in the window pane. The chair placed diagonally in the corner, with lions' heads on the uprights, defines the angle of the room whose space is a magnetic field where figure and surrounding objects are held together in an all-embracing tension. The color scheme, built up around a few dense and sober tones of gray, brown, green and yellow, is broken by a nascent "pointillism." Here, for the first time, Vermeer takes possession of his secret realm of evasion, illusion, and allusion, of "dreaming calm and utter immobility pervaded with an elegiac clarity too delicate to be described as melancholy" (Huizinga).

The "Girl in Blue reading a Letter" (about 1665, Rijksmuseum, Amsterdam), much admired by Van Gogh and surely one of the supreme achievements of the painter's art, marks the fulfillment of the promise contained in the Dresden picture. Vermeer has found his perfect form: a monumental figure steeped in light. Modulations of blue against the yellowish brown of the map on the back wall throw into focus the creamy tones of the face, and of the hands holding the white sheet of paper. With Vermeer, as with Terborch, woman's place is at the heart of the picture, either alone or attended by the maidservant who, in democratic Holland, was one of the family and shared her mistress's secrets.

Jan Vermeer (1632-1675). Lady standing at the Virginals, about 1671. (20¼ × 17¾")
By Courtesy of the Trustees, National Gallery, London.

The slightly later "Lady writing a Letter" (about 1670, Sir Alfred Beit Collection, London) cannot quite equal the rapt suspense suggested by the "Girl in Blue" (we reproduce the two pictures side by side), but in it Vermeer's technical mastery reaches its zenith. The pose of the letter writer is substantially that of the "Lacemaker" (Louvre), reversed, with the same plenitude of form, the same elusive flicker of lights and shadows, and that ineffable mildness of tone and mood which, as in Chardin, results from a sound, unequivocal color harmony. It was this that prompted Thoré-Bürger to call Vermeer "an enamelist of genius," and Jan Veth to describe his tones as "a fusion of ground pearls." And the pearl indeed, so often worn by the women in his pictures, symbolizes Vermeer so perfectly—just as gold, glowing in the depths of shadow, symbolizes Rembrandt—that each drop of color distilled by his brush seems to assume on canvas the volume and coloration of orient pearls.

The same pair of women—mistress and maid, Martha and Mary—reappear, again brought together by a letter, in two roughly contemporary pictures (Frick Collection, New York, and Rijksmuseum, Amsterdam) which are charged, however, with different intentions. In a recent study of "Vermeer's Musical Subjects" (in the "Gazette des Beaux-Arts," January 1961) which occur in twelve out of thirty-one extant paintings (and occur several times in conjunction with the letter theme), the French connoisseur A.P. de Mirimonde throws a good deal of new light on the meaning and implications of pictures whose fascination we feel at once, though hitherto no one has been able to explain exactly what the subject is. Thus the letter being written by a young woman seated at a table, in a painting datable to about 1665 (formerly Lady Oakes Collection, Nassau, Bahamas), should be interpreted as an invitation to a musical party. This is suggested indirectly by a picture within the picture, a still life hanging on the wall behind the letter writer and representing a bass viol, or viola da gamba. The tender, muffled sonority of this instrument made it ideal for accompanying the harpsichord or the virginals, which were to be found in every well-to-do home in Vermeer's time. In the refined, pleasure-loving society of seventeenth century Holland, chamber music was a favorite pastime, and a favorite pretext for a social gathering, a gay party, a love duet. To receive her partner, the lady musician donned all her finery, as the lady has done in this picture, almost flaunting her fine array, whose rather showy elegance marks her as a woman of loose character, though one, nevertheless, of a certain distinction who makes a point of keeping up appearances. The Dutch historian Johan Huizinga, with his usual discernment, noticed this feature of Vermeer's work and commented on it. "The truth is," he wrote, "that these women in yellow, blue or green house-jackets are not the wives of patricians, burghers, or merchants. They seem to belong to an unavowed demi-monde." As in France in the next century, music and painting were united in rich plastic combinations full of ambiguous allusions and innuendoes.

In the light of the foregoing remarks, the later companion pieces, "A Lady seated at the Virginals" and "A Lady standing at the Virginals" (about 1671, National Gallery, London), hitherto deemed enigmatic, are seen to be pretty clear in meaning. For in the first, sure enough, we find a bass viol standing beside the virginals in readiness for the young woman's expected visitor; and above, hanging on the wall, is "The Procuress" by Theodor van Baburen, a picture owned by Vermeer which also figures in "The Concert" (about 1662, Boston Museum of Fine Arts). The second, which we reproduce, shows a rather bold-eyed young woman, dressed in the French fashion, standing at the virginals in a cube-shaped room and impatiently *running her fingers along the keyboard. On the wall behind her hangs a large picture of Cupid (which reappears in "A Girl Asleep" and "A Girl interrupted at Music" in New York) triumphantly holding aloft the letter which the lady musician, or pretended musician, has just received. This time the allusion is so direct that there is no need of a second instrument to hint at the imminent arrival of her partner.*

As for the famous "Love Letter" (about 1669, Rijksmuseum, Amsterdam), so skillfully composed and elaborately contrived, it may well be that the title is a misnomer. Judging by the look of things, and the hints contained in the picture, this is no love letter; it is on the contrary a letter of estrangement. The lady of the house, neglecting her domestic duties and dressed in her Sunday best, with pearl earrings and pearl necklace, has been fingering her lute to beguile the time while waiting. She had a rendezvous with an accompanyist who has failed to appear. Instead a message has come, and as the maidservant hands it to her we read surprise and vexation on her face and in her upturned eyes. The two pictures on the back wall make it sufficiently clear what the letter contains: above, under the looped-up drapery over the doorway, is a landscape showing a man with his back turned, walking away; below is a ship in a rough sea, the usual symbol of inconstancy in the books of emblems to which Vermeer often referred for his motifs.

True enough, as André Malraux says of this picture, "the letter has no importance, nor have the women. Nor has the world in which letters are delivered: that world has been transmuted into painting." But for us it has been thus transmuted only since Manet and Cézanne, and a better understanding of the picture's subject, and of the meaning it actually had for Vermeer's contemporaries, takes away nothing of its indefinable fascination as a pure work of art.

Jan Vermeer (1632-1675). The "Love Letter," about 1669.
(17¼×15⅛″) Rijksmuseum, Amsterdam.

Pieter de Hooch (1629-1684?). Interior with a Young Woman reading a Letter.
(22⅜×18⅞″) National Museum, Stockholm.

This is the only painting by Vermeer, together with "A Girl Asleep" (Metropolitan Museum, New York), in which a door in the foreground opens on another room behind—a favorite device of Pieter de Hooch (1629-1684?). The unbridgeable gulf between style and story-telling, between poetry and prose, is what separates Vermeer—"a humming-bird among sparrows," as Friedländer described him—from all his intimist contemporaries. Nevertheless it would be a mistake to belittle the talent and charm of Pieter de Hooch, the best of them all after Terborch. Born at Rotterdam, he settled at Delft in 1653 and in the following year married the daughter of a local potter. The happiness of his home life, the climate of taste in Delft, so propitious to young, talented painters, and his friendly rivalry with Vermeer, all stimulated his creative powers. In these years he revealed the best of himself, before he made an ill-advised move to Amsterdam, where his art steadily deteriorated.

De Hooch's principal letter pictures, however, were painted during the early phase of his Amsterdam period. While they fail to sustain the quality of his Delft work, there are still some excellent pictures among them. The "Billet Doux" (Museum of Fine Arts, Budapest) is dated 1664, and the "Messenger" (Rijksmuseum, Amsterdam) 1670. To about the same year can be assigned the Hamburg picture, another version of the Budapest theme, which he later reverted to again in the New York "Love Letter" (1680) and in the Stockholm painting which we reproduce. A young woman in a bright red mantlet and a white satin skirt is reading, with languid attention though her curiosity is aroused, what seems to be an unexpected message, while a blue-habited cavalier leans on the window sill and gazes into the street. The bright colors stand out in the foreground against a dark background pierced by an open door. Not for him were the cool, limpid color schemes which seem to have been the inimitable privilege of Vermeer (and of Piero della Francesca). He fell back accordingly on the warm, golden harmonies, blending a sense of intimacy with deeper intimations, that we find in Aelbert Cuyp's landscapes and in Emanuel de Witte's church interiors. In contrast with the ostentation of the Amsterdam school to which Pieter de Hooch increasingly yielded, the theme of the letter in painting was discreetly carried on in the Delft tradition by several charmingly sensitive little masters, like Pieter Janssens Elinga ("The Messenger," about 1675, National Gallery, Oslo).

Sebastian Stoskopff (1597-1657). Still Life with Basket of Glasses, Pâté and Letter. (19½×25″)
Musée des Beaux-Arts, Strasbourg.

44

2

*N*o independent still life by Vermeer has survived. Yet, if we are really entitled to speak of a "still life spirit" as the profoundest characteristic of Dutch painting, that spirit is better embodied by Vermeer and the intimist school of Delft than by the innumerable specialists of still life painting in seventeenth century Holland. While its origins go back to antiquity, the still life as an art form first emerged in the fifteenth century, and has enjoyed in our own time a great return to favor, with Cézanne, the Cubists and the Surrealists. Its heyday, however, came in the seventeenth century. The rise of still life painting in Holland, like that of landscape, was largely due to the desire felt by the men of that day to transform and humanize their environment, to make themselves, as Descartes expressed it at the time, "masters and possessors of nature." This desire was implicit in the outlook on life of a realistic-minded, middle-class society founded on the free exchange of goods, a society accustomed to assessing things in the light of their practical utility and market value. While the Dutch still life reflected all this, at the same time a precise allegorical or symbolical meaning was attached to every item in the picture.

The repertory of still life painting has varied little throughout the centuries, consisting always of a limited number of familiar objects accompanying man through life, serving his needs and ministering to his pleasures.

It may be roughly divided into two categories: (1) still life of a sensuous character, flowers, fruit, food and the dishes containing it, grouped on a table and representing the different meals of the day, and even particular phases of a meal; and (2) still life of an intellectual character, books, musical instruments, attributes of the arts and sciences, emblems of material wealth and temporal power, which the flight of time and the fatality of death, symbolized by a skull, a guttering candle or an hourglass, transform into vain and transient possessions—and so these were often called Vanitas pictures.

While still lifes containing books and musical instruments with scores occur frequently, from the Primitives to the Cubists, still lifes with letters are much rarer. Letters and inkstands occasionally figure in Vanitas pictures. There also exists a series of seventeenth century still lifes in which, amid heterogeneous objects, a letter is visible, inscribed with the painter's name and address. The best and most famous example, dated 1630, is a still life in the Spada Gallery in Rome with a signed letter in it, which revealed the painter to be the enigmatic Baugin (not even his Christian name is known), one of the great masters of French still life painting. The same device was often used in portraits, though here, as a rule, it was the model's name and title, if any, that were written on a letter held in his hand or placed well in view on a table.

The allegorical still life contained objects symbolizing either the five senses or the vanity of earthly things. The two were combined in the work of a rival of Baugin: Sebastian Stoskopff (1597-1657) of Strasbourg, a complex and compelling artist who united, as few others have done, a sharpness of linear definition and a Germanic sense of mystery with an exemplary rigor and purity that are typically French. His "Still Life with Basket of Glasses, Pâté and Letter" belongs to the best phase of his Paris period, when Stoskopff was living at Saint-Germain-des-Prés, center of a thriving colony of Northern artists and of the French school known as Painters of Reality. Standing out against a uniform, abstract background of blue black is a wickerwork basket full of empty glasses flashing with reflected light—a favorite theme of this artist (a notorious tippler), who painted glasses with many variations in his later pictures. The basket stands on a heavy wooden table, of brown and ochre streaked with white. Under a large succulent meat pie, liberally partaken of already, lies an unfolded letter, its red seal striking the only resonant note in a sober and delicate color scheme. The handwriting of the letter is illegible, but the address distinctly reads: "Monsieur Teniers." This no doubt refers to the Flemish painter David Teniers the Elder (1582-1649), who was also an art dealer, and with whom Stoskopff certainly had dealings, either in Paris or Antwerp. Two still lifes by Juan Gris (1887-1927), dated 1926, also contain unfolded letters, but with no writing visible on them, one lying flat under a carafe and a fruit dish, the other under a bottle and a pair of scissors.

"Trompe-l'oeil" (i.e. illusionism so cunningly contrived as to deceive the eye into taking the painted object for the real thing) has always been the aim and the pitfall of figurative painting based on the principle of nature imitation, and this is especially true of still life painting. In the hands of most painters "trompe-l'oeil" is a mere technical feat, usually devoid of genuine artistic merit. On the other hand, it was a device by no means disdained by artists of the caliber of Vermeer and Chardin, and under their brush its limitations were magically overcome and transcended.

We reproduce together two significant examples of illusionist painting, one by a French painter, one by an American, both composed almost entirely of letters, and separated in time by an interval of two centuries.

Wallerand Vaillant (1623-1677). Letters with Quill and Penknife, 1658.
(20¼×16″) Gemäldegalerie, Dresden.

John Frederick Peto (1854-1907). Old Scraps, 1894. (30×25⅛″)
Collection Museum of Modern Art, New York. Gift of Nelson A. Rockefeller.

Born at Lille in 1623, Wallerand Vaillant received his training in Antwerp, worked for a time in Frankfort, and died in Amsterdam in 1677. He is best known as a portrait painter and engraver. Attention was first attracted to his "Letters with Quill and Penknife" (Gemälde-galerie, Dresden) when it was shown in Paris in 1934 at the exhibition of Painters of Reality. The illusionism of this curious picture, of Dutch inspiration disciplined by an orderly French layout, extends even to the date (1658), which appears to be chalked on one of the boards, with carefully simulated graining, which act as the background. Tacked to the boards are strips of red ribbon forming a geometric pattern and conveniently holding eight or ten letters, a goose quill and a small knife for cutting and mending quill pens. Sober browns, light grays and dull reds are discreetly relieved by the brighter accents of the seals. Several addresses are perfectly legible, one in German, the others in French. The folded letter on the lower left bears the painter's signature: "Wallerand Vaillant fecit."

Illusionist painting, whether the work of real artists or, more often, of skilled craftsmen, enjoyed its greatest vogue in eighteenth century Europe, appealing to both aristocratic and popular tastes, serving a decorative purpose and answering at the same time to the prevailing esthetic of illusion and make-believe. This tradition of "trompe-l'oeil" painting died out in France with Louis-Léopold Boilly (1761-1845), but it was transplanted to the United States where it lingered on until the end of the nineteenth century, adapted to the tastes of a young middle-class society which took a naive delight in the literal naturalism of this art.

Its American sponsor was the School of Philadelphia, founded by Raphaelle Peale (1774-1825), whose best known representative however was William Harnett (1848-1892). Harnett enjoyed an extraordinary vogue in the 1880's, his pictures fetching as much as $10,000 apiece. Then he fell into oblivion, only to be resuscitated a few years ago on the strength of a fancied kinship with the Surrealists. He liked to fill his still lifes with a choice selection of objects, often rare books and valuable musical instruments, represented in "trompe-l'oeil" in a crystalline style of linear precision. His signature is sometimes introduced in the guise of stamped and postmarked letters bearing his name and address. So great was the success of these works that many fakes appeared on the market; twenty or so of the best of them have recently been recognized as pictures that were actually the work of John Frederick Peto (1854-1907), another Philadelphia painter and apparently a friend of Harnett's. One of these is reproduced here: "Old Scraps" (Museum of Modern Art, New York), painted in 1894, two years after the death of Harnett, whose signature had been cleverly forged on the painting over the genuine signature of Peto.

Harnett had studied in Europe for several years, chiefly in Munich, where he acquired a professional academic training. Peto was self-taught and earned a meager livelihood as a photographer and postcard designer, selling his paintings for paltry sums. About 1880 he began imitating Harnett, though in a very personal way, with a freer, softer handling of the brush, and with color schemes and lighting faintly reminiscent at times of Vermeer. Peto, long before Kurt Schwitters and the Surrealists, discovered the poetic charm of outworn, discarded objects. Significantly composed, like that of Wallerand Vaillant, Peto's "trompe-l'oeil" still life represents strips of felt holding a motley assortment of objects against a wooden door: several envelopes (with the postmarks clearly legible), two books or notebooks, a faded snapshot, a goose quill, together with a bit of string, a torn label, scraps of printed matter, and a column of chalk-written figures.

From the postal point of view, two important innovations are visible here, both of which appeared in the nineteenth century: the postal envelope (hitherto, as shown in Vaillant's picture, a letter consisted simply of a folded sheet, sealed on one side and addressed on the other) and the postage stamp (first issued in England in 1840, in the United States in 1845, and in France in 1849). Postage stamps later figured occasionally in the "papiers collés" (pasted papers) of the Cubists, coming by then as both the climax and the overthrow of illusionist painting.

The roll-top desk known as the Desk of King Stanislaus (now in the Wallace Collection, London) is a slightly simplified variant of the famous Desk of King Louis XV, the "Bureau du Roi" at Versailles, perhaps the masterpiece of French cabinetmaking. Presumably both were ordered at the same time by the queen, Marie Leczinska, for her father and her husband. They were designed and begun, it seems, by J. F. Oeben (1721-1763) and finished by J. H. Riesener (1734-1806). The elaborate marquetry work, both inside and out, includes flower patterns, the emblems of France and Poland, the attributes of the Sciences, the Arts and Letters. The pictorial inlays of wood are based on similar Italian works of the fifteenth century, which lie at the origin both of the independent still life and of the "trompe-l'oeil" picture. Such inlays were a common feature of fine furniture between 1760 and 1780.

The upper panel of the Desk of King Stanislaus, of which we illustrate a detail, is an illusionist still life of writing materials, including two written pages skillfully incised in the wood. The lefthand page bears the signature of the cabinetmaker, J. H. Riesener, and the date of February 20, 1769, when the desk was probably finished. The righthand page is more difficult to read; beginning with the formal salutation "Monsieur" and continuing in

German, it is usually interpreted as a letter from Marie Leczinska to her father Stanislaus, the ill-fated king of Poland living in exile at Nancy, to whom she was devoted. As Stanislaus died in 1766 and the queen in 1768, neither lived to see the completion of the desk.

The eighteenth century brought to perfection the standard varieties of writing tables, from the plain flat desk to the most elaborate type of bureau or escritoire, with its drawers, cupboards and pigeon-holes. And the same century consecrated the triumph of letter writing, both as a literary form and as a theme for painters.

Jean-Henri Riesener (1734-1806). The Desk of King Stanislaus, 1769. Detail of the Marquetry.
Wallace Collection, London.

Jean-Baptiste-Siméon Chardin (1699-1779). Lady sealing a Letter, 1733. (56¾×56¾″) Staatliche Museen, Berlin-Dahlem.

The 18th Century

3

Oddly enough, if the first Vermeer really corresponding to our idea of Vermeer is the "Young Woman reading a Letter" in Dresden, it so happens that the first Chardin in which his genius asserts itself is the "Lady sealing a Letter" from the royal palace at Potsdam. A big square canvas, signed and dated 1733, "his largest figure composition and one of the finest pieces of painting in the world" (Louis Gillet), it may have been intended to commemorate the artist's marriage in 1731 with Marguerite Saintard. Seated at a writing table covered with a garnet-red table-carpet with blue and yellow borders, a fashionable young woman dressed in a dark blue gown and a striped wrapper, seen in profile as she turns away, is holding in one hand a letter finished but a moment before (she has just laid down her quill beside the inkstand), and in the other a stick of red sealing wax. Standing deferentially behind the table, leaning slightly forward, a footman is lighting the candle, while a dog is frisking at the feet of its mistress. A heavy curtain in the background has been drawn aside, showing the bare walls of the room.

The Dutch influences so conspicuous in Chardin's previous work have here been absorbed, and the earlier atmosphere of anecdote and dalliance dissolved in an utterly silent, motionless concentration of purely pictorial qualities combining the moral resonance of Lenain with the saturated colors of Vermeer, to which Chardin gives an even deeper warmth of tone.

François Guérin (1735?-1791). Lady reading a Letter beside a Child. Pastel. (9⅝ × 11¼″) Albertina, Vienna.

Chardin perhaps gave away something of his secret when he said, "One doesn't paint with colors but with feelings." Yet he was the master of a technique whose perfection can be seen in the making in this very fine early work—a technique thus described by a contemporary chronicler, Louis de Bachaumont: "He lays in his colors one after the other without blending them, with the result that his work is not unlike a mosaic." By boldly juxtaposing his colors and hardly mixing them at all, Chardin achieved that

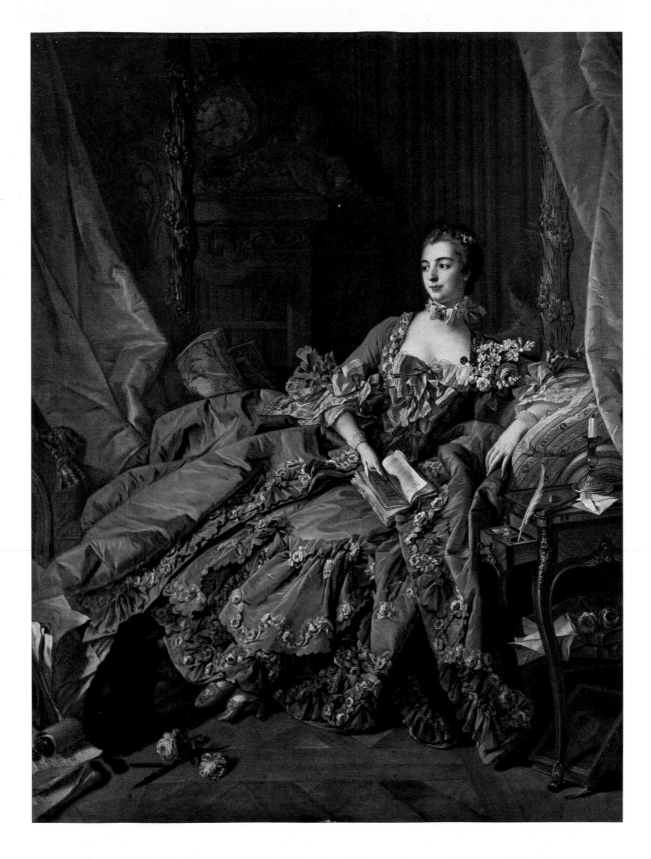

François Boucher (1703-1770). The Marquise de Pompadour, 1758. Private Collection.

shimmering, variegated texture which enables light and air to circulate freely and makes shadows transparent. There exist several replicas and copies of the "Lady sealing a Letter," notably by Beaujon and Hubert Robert, and the picture was a great favorite with printmakers throughout the eighteenth and nineteenth centuries.

Of humble origin, the son of a tiler, Watteau (1684-1721) opened the century and lived to become the prince of painters in the Regency period, between the reigns of Louis XIV and Louis XV, creating a dreamworld of shadow-dappled glades and strolling couples, of carefree "fêtes galantes" and costumed players from the French and Italian Comedy. But he died young: the revels ended, the pageant faded, and left not a rack behind. And the art of Watteau's successors evolved on different lines. Chardin, son of a cabinetmaker, was an impassive observer of the daily round of bourgeois life. A unique blend of Nordic gravity and French grace, his art formed as it were a stable point of equilibrium between the two poles of eighteenth century French painting, Boucher (1703-1770) and Fragonard (1732-1806). On Chardin converged—and flowed from him afresh, quickened and deepened—the currents of reality underlying the artifice and glitter of his lesser contemporaries.

Among the many ferments of an effervescent period rich in contrasts, disguising under fancy dress its obstinate quest of the natural (and, a little later, of nature), the dominant factor is first of all the "free spirit," well-spring of new and increasingly subversive ideas. The vivacity of the eighteenth century mind sprang from a passionate heart bridled by reason, and under a veneer of propriety it gave rise to bold liberties untainted either by cynicism or vulgarity. It enlivened conversation, the supreme art of a refined, cosmopolitan society, which believed in good manners and delighted in the give-and-take of good talk. Sprightly wit bubbled over in drawing rooms, crackled and burst in cafés and clubs, sharpened the point of epigrams and maxims, spiced and inspired comedies, tales and novels. Dialogue became, as never before, an effective vehicle of literary expression in the hands of Rousseau, Voltaire and Diderot, who were all delightful letter writers, and the two outstanding French novels of the century, "La Nouvelle Héloïse" (1761) and "Les Liaisons Dangereuses" (1782), are composed entirely of letters, following the example of Richardson in England.

Writings of all kinds, topical or imaginative, official or private, European or exotic, now took an epistolary form, from the "Lettres à l'Académie" (1714) of Fénelon to the "Lettres à Sophie" (1792) of Mirabeau, and including the "Lettres Persanes" (1721) of Montesquieu, the "Lettres Anglaises" (1734) of Voltaire and the "Lettres Familières" (1740) written from Italy by Charles de Brosses, not to mention the letters of the Prince de Ligne and Mademoiselle de Lespinasse, those of Madame du Deffand to Horace Walpole, and the correspondence, still in part unpublished (and unpublishable), of Beaumarchais, the happy-go-lucky creator of Figaro and the Barber of Seville.

The first gazettes and newspapers were then making their appearance, some in the form of hand-written news letters, retailing the gossip and tabletalk of the town, sent by the post to members and frequenters of a particular social circle. Every pretext was good to open or keep up a correspondence, and no other word in fact could better symbolize the ideal of easy and courteous social and intellectual relations that held sway in the Europe of that day, which Paul Valéry recognized as, all in all, "the best of possible worlds," for "there was room enough for wayward fancies and standards were strict enough without being cramping." The rising volume of letters passing through

Jean-Etienne Liotard (1702-1789). Portrait of Mademoiselle Lavergne, 1746. Pastel. (20½ × 16½″)
Rijksmuseum, Amsterdam.

Jean Raoux (1677-1734). Girl reading a Letter. (31½×39⅜″) Louvre, Paris.

the mails, further increased by the passion for travel and the development of commerce and industry, led to an international reorganization of the postal system and to the creation of district post offices for the daily collection and delivery of letters within a given locality.

Like literature and music, and often in combination with the latter, as in Holland, painting embodied the spirit of the age, its fickle and buoyant enthusiasms, its impassioned temperament. Never had painting been more spontaneously pictorial, or handled with more freedom and brio, and never had painters been more enamored of color. As for portraitists and genre painters, stimulated by the example of the Dutch, and their environment being what it was, it was only natural for them to turn to epistolary themes. The initiator in France was J.B. Santerre (1651-1717) who, in the twilight of the long reign of Louis XIV, created both the fanciful portrait and the realistic portrait. His "Woman sealing a Letter" and "Woman dispatching a Letter" have both disappeared unfortunately, but the theme was taken up by Alexis Grimou (1678-1723) and above all by Jean Raoux (1677-1734), who adapted the Dutch letter picture to Parisian tastes and treated it on a larger scale. Raoux painted a "Girl surprised by her Grandmother while reading a Letter" (Marseilles Museum), a "Girl sealing a Letter" (Béziers Museum), and the charming "Girl reading a Letter" (Louvre, Paris), shown in three-quarter view to the right, holding the page up to an unseen light. Wearing a yellow dress with full sleeves and a blue, beribboned bodice laced over a low-necked chemisette, she is softly modeled in light and shadow, by contrasting tones and subtle shadings punctuated with fleeting gleams.

As a pendant to this picture we illustrate the "Portrait of Mademoiselle Lavergne" (Rijksmuseum, Amsterdam), by the half French, half Genevese painter Jean-Etienne Liotard (1702-1789). The young lady, who was

Liotard's niece, has taken the same pose in reverse and is similarly dressed, in a blue, embroidered bodice tightly laced over a chemisette or shift, above a full, light gray skirt. This portrait is a pastel, a rapid technique of particular delicacy and precision, and one that was a great favorite with eighteenth century painters. Signed and dated 1746, the picture was executed at Lyons, in the course of one of the artist's journeys from Geneva to Paris. The small crucifix on a black string—in contrast with the pearl necklace in Raoux's portrait—tempers the splendor of the costume with a Puritan note. There exists a preliminary sketch of the picture in the Dresden Gallery.

Boucher, the greatest decorator of the century, produced a vast body of work, now broken up and dispersed, which for the most part goes unappreciated today. Yet this accomplished and versatile artist was a landscapist, genre painter and portraitist of great natural charm. Of his devoted patron, Madame de Pompadour, of whom he was not only the painter in ordinary, but the acknowledged friend and counsellor, he left many portraits, both in oils and pastels, seated or standing; the finest are those in the National Gallery of Scotland, Edinburgh, the Wallace Collection, London, and another in a private collection. The latter in particular, dated 1758, is a magnificent work, beautifully designed and exquisitely colored. It is aptly described by the French scholar and historian Pierre de Nolhac, who was probably more at home in eighteenth century France than anyone since the Goncourt brothers.

"Madame de Pompadour is seated on a sofa, with a book in her hand, wearing a blue silk gown embroidered with roses running along the trimmings and the double flounces, from which emerge a dainty pair of high-heeled shoes. Her bodice is a cascade of mauve-colored ribbons, and a similar ribbon encircles her neck. There are flowers in her hair, a bouquet pinned to her

Jean-Honoré Fragonard (1732-1806). The Letter. (15 × 11⅝″)
Mr. and Mrs. Charles W. Engelhard, Newark, N. J.

breast, and six rows of pearls to her bracelets. The furniture is most interesting. The Marquise has just finished writing a letter, which is still lying beside the candle, the seal and the stick of sealing wax on the small rosewood table, whose open drawer contains a quill and inkstand. Under the table, on the floor, lies a beautifully bound volume; on the other side, scattered at her feet, are a portfolio of drawings, a pencil-holder and a graving needle —an ostentatious display, flattering her artistic pretensions, which even La Tour made a point of including in his portrait of her. On the floor, two roses and the inevitable pug-dog. Behind her, framed on either side by yellow damask curtains and the trunks of palm trees, a large looking glass reflects a low bookcase, more ornate than those in earlier portraits and surmounted by a richly wrought clock, crowned with a bronze lyre and flanked by recumbent Cupids. As usual everything is neatly contrived to show the Marquise in the familiar setting of her daily life."

The Marquise de Pompadour, who virtually governed France in the reign of Louis XV, making and unmaking the king's ministers and actually shaping the nation's foreign policy, also played a decisive part in the evolution of decorative art and furniture styles. She was influential above all in the development of the many different types of writing cabinets, writing desks and writing tables: secretaires, bureaux, escritoires, chiffoniers, and the charmingly named "bonheur-du-jour" (a lady's writing desk) whose special characteristic is a raised back, forming a small cabinet or a nest of drawers, or simply fitted with a mirror, thus doing duty as a dressing table. Though the demand for these articles of furniture was bound up with the rise and spread of letter writing, she made them fashionable and personally encouraged their manufacture. And they number among the most attractive and consummate works of this Golden Age of French cabinetmaking.

Chardin, a pure painter, like Vermeer, has left very few drawings. Two charming pastels, "Lady writing a Letter" and "Lady reading a Letter beside a Child" (both in the Albertina, Vienna), were long attributed to him on the strength of inscriptions, and by reason too of their high quality. But they now appear to be the work of François Guérin (1735?-1791), a pupil of Natoire, who enjoyed a certain amount of success at the Salons of 1761 and 1763, and whose pictures were eagerly collected. The one we reproduce has been thought to be an intimate glimpse of Madame de Pompadour and her daughter, in the privacy of her boudoir, without (for once) the pomp and trappings of her "official" portraits.

All the letters so attentively read, written or sealed by these elegant young women are—it goes without saying—love letters or "billets doux." For affairs of the heart, from the mildest flirting to rakish libertinage, were the great concern of the period, catered to by music and dancing, by the theater, and by the rage for parlor games. The theme of the love letter, already treated by Boucher, was taken up by his brilliant pupil Fragonard, whose virtuoso bravura and bold versatility must not blind us to his sterling qualities as a painter and poet, to which the Goncourt brothers and the Impressionists, Renoir in particular, paid admiring tribute. In 1771, for the famous pavilion of Madame du Barry, at Louveciennes, who by now had replaced La Pompadour in the affections of the aging king, he painted a set of four panels picturing "The Progress of Love" (unaccountably rejected by the royal favorite and now in the Frick Collection, New York). The third and most famous panel is "The Love Letter": in the sunny clearing of a wooded park, the happy lover has seated his mistress on a marble altar and holds her tenderly by the waist as she glances down at one of the letters they have exchanged.

Jean-Honoré Fragonard (1732-1806). The Billet Doux. (32¾×26⅜″)
Courtesy of The Metropolitan Museum of Art, New York. The Jules S. Bache Collection, 1949.

Pietro Longhi (1702-1785). The Moorish Messenger. (24×19⅝″) Ca' Rezzonico, Venice.

From 1775 to 1777, when he returned to Paris from his second trip to Italy, Fragonard reverted several times to this theme, handling it now with a more intimate and natural touch. For he was in love himself—with his pretty sister-in-law Marguerite Gérard, twenty years his junior, who had become his pupil and favorite model. A correspondence sprang up between them, of which all that survive are Marguerite's tender but evasive replies to the eager advances of the incurable libertine. It was this infatuation, perhaps, that led him to paint in rapid succession a series of studies, some of them now lost, of young women, smiling, pouting or peeved, deep in the perusal of a love letter. Among the best is "The Letter," sometimes called "Memories" (Mr. and Mrs. Charles W. Engelhard, Newark), which once belonged to the beautiful Madame Récamier. A masterpiece of tremulous intimacy and sheer pictorial verve, it harks back to Frans Hals and at the same time points toward Renoir. The famous "Billet Doux" (Metropolitan Museum, New York) represents a young woman seated at her writing table, beside a fluffy lap dog, and archly glancing at us over her shoulder. Wearing a blue dressing gown and a beribboned bonnet, she is slipping a message into a bouquet of flowers. The superscription has been variously interpreted; some read "Monsieur Mon Cavalier," others "A Monsieur Cuvillier." If the latter name were correct, then the model would be Boucher's daughter, Marie Emilie, widow of the painter Beaudoin, who in 1773 married a Monsieur Cuvillier.

Pictures on epistolary themes were very much in demand throughout the period. At the official Salon of 1777 several were exhibited by the young painters P.A. Wille (1748-1821) and Anne Vallayer-Coster (1744-1818). Fragonard went on exploiting them, notably in an incomparable set of wash drawings, the finest of which is the "Spanish Conversation" (Art Institute of Chicago). And we find them drawn or engraved, with various shades of equivocal innuendoes, in the work of all the chroniclers and little masters of the century, Beaudoin, Carmontelle, Saint-Aubin, Janin, Debucourt, and a host of others.

A superb black chalk drawing (1772, Valence Museum), the initial sketch for a painting inspired by Chardin's "Lady sealing a Letter," reveals an unexpected aspect of the landscape painter Hubert Robert (1733-1808), a friend of Fragonard's and his travel companion in Italy. The drawing shows Madame Geoffrin writing a letter in her study, while a periwigged footman snuffs the candles above the fireplace. Seen from behind, she is seated at her desk, above which hangs a painting by Vien. Furnishings have changed since the days of Madame de Pompadour; here we have the chaste simplicity of the Louis XVI style. Although of humble origin and of no great culture, Madame Geoffrin, from 1744 to her death in 1777, presided over one of the leading literary and artistic circles in Paris. She gave two dinners a week: on Monday for artists, on Wednesday for men of letters. She corresponded with King Stanislaus of Poland, and in her drawing room received David Hume, Edward Gibbon, Horace Walpole and many other celebrities visiting or passing through Paris.

French taste, French fashions and the universality of the French language made Paris the capital of Europe in the eighteenth century, but London and Venice could almost rival her. As far as painting is concerned, Venice actually outrivaled Paris. Failing to make his mark in the monumental painting so brilliantly illustrated by Tiepolo, Pietro Longhi (1702-1785) turned to genre scenes and small-scale pictures, chronicling Venetian life and society under many different aspects. The documentary value of his work tends to make us overlook both its high pictorial quality and the light

Thomas Gainsborough (1727-1788). Portrait of Mrs. John Douglas, 1784.
Waddesdon Manor (National Trust), near Aylesbury, Buckinghamshire.

social comedy so often implicit in it. A subtle colorist, delighting in mellow, finely shaded harmonies, his ironical detachment from the frivolities of the time and place he lived in has its counterpart in the comedies of his friend Goldoni. Longhi's most fruitful period is that of his middle years, round about 1750, when he turned out a string of masterpieces remarkable for the bloom of their colors and the lilting grace of the figure groups. Among them are two pictures on letter themes: "The Letter" (Metropolitan Museum, New York) and "The Moorish Messenger" (Ca' Rezzonico, Venice). From the mosaics of St. Mark's to Longhi, by way of Carpaccio, Veronese and others, Moors and Negroes often appear in Venetian art. By the eighteenth century, colored servants had become common, not only in Venice but throughout Europe, because of their exotic appearance, their fidelity and devotion, and their usefulness as private messengers who—as they could neither read nor write—could safely be trusted with confidential letters.

The best Dutch portraitist and genre painter of the period was Cornelis Troost (1697-1750), who sometimes took over the epistolary themes of his great predecessors in Holland, but always in a spirit more akin to that of William Hogarth (1697-1764), the English creator of satirical story-pictures with a moral purpose, a type of art that spread to the continent in the latter part of the eighteenth century. The real strength of the English School, however, lay in romantic and aristocratic portraiture, as derived from Van Dyck, and even more in landscape painting inspired by Northern models and answering to that growing sensitiveness to natural beauty which, at the same period, found expression in the poetry of Gray and Cowper.

Thomas Gainsborough (1727-1788) not only practiced portraiture and landscape separately and was a decisive innovator in both; he also combined them successfully in open-air portraits no less characteristic of the English *sensibility than the drawing-room portrait was of French taste. The full-length portraits of women made in his final London period, for which the great collectors have always bidded eagerly at the highest prices, are sometimes belittled by critics; yet they number among the artist's most felicitous works. This is certainly the case with the "Portrait of Mrs. John Douglas" (1784, Waddesdon Manor, near Aylesbury, Bucks). The fashionably dressed young woman is absorbed, with graceful artlessness, in the perusal of a letter, and the garden setting is perfectly attuned to her pensive mood. The fine free handling of the paints, the musical overtones of the colors, and the easy, lyrical expression of feeling are already unreservedly romantic. While at times recalling Fragonard and even Watteau, Gainsborough points the way to Constable (who made no secret of what he owed him) and also to Goya (whom he foreshadows in certain spirited accents, as Roger Fry has observed) —to the two opposing masters, that is, who brought the eighteenth century to a close and ushered in the nineteenth.*

Francisco Goya (1746-1828). Majas walking on the Banks of the Manzanares, 1814-1816. (71¼×48″)
Palais des Beaux-Arts, Lille.

4

*W*hile the renewal of landscape painting based on natural vision, which made it the paramount art form in Europe from 1820 to 1880, was the pioneer contribution of England, and of Constable (1776-1837) in particular, it was Spain, in the person of Goya (1746-1828), that founded modern humanism. Breaking with the pageantry and make-believe of eighteenth century art, Goya tore off the mask, defied convention, and confronted man with the lonely and naked image of himself.

His long career is marked by an unbroken succession of both intimate and official portraits of writers, diplomats, ministers, doctors, etc., holding a letter in their hand or seated at their writing desk; others are shown in half length against an abstract background, with no accessories, or in full length against the open sky. These works testify to an ever keener insight into the model's inner life and an ever bolder handling of the brush. But it was above all in his genre pictures, of a kind never seen before, that he scaled the heights. One of the finest is in the Lille museum: "Majas walking on the Banks of the Manzanares" or "Young People" (it forms a pendant with another picture in the same museum entitled "Old People"). Datable to 1814-1816 and thus contemporary with some of Goya's most tragic visions and with a dazzling series of portraits and self-portraits, this picture reverts, in a different key and with broader rhythms, to the themes of his early work.

Elisabeth Vigée-Lebrun (1755-1842). Lady folding a Letter, 1784. (36½×29½″) Private Collection.

Jacques-Louis David (1748-1825). Portrait of Alexandre Lenoir, 1817. (29⅞×24⅜″) Louvre, Paris.

Two young women strolling along the Manzanares, in the suburbs of Madrid, have paused for a moment. One, strikingly dressed in black and white, with a filmy white mantilla enclosing the perfect oval of her face and setting off her handsome, sensuous features, is drawing herself up proudly, with her left hand on her hip, and reading a letter held almost at arm's length in her right hand, while her terrier yaps at her feet and clamors for attention. A tight-fitting bodice adds a provocative note to her ample charms. Her companion in a black mantilla and a tobacco-colored robe—no doubt her maid—gracefully swings her hip as she opens a large yellow parasol to screen her mistress from the sun, whose heat can be gauged by the heavy shadows cast on the ground.

Forming a complete contrast with these two idle and haughty beauties jauntily posed under a sultry sky intenser than a Manet, the background of the picture represents a busy group of washerwomen huddled on the river bank. These figures and the laundry drying behind them are boldly sketched in compact masses prefiguring Daumier.

Official painter first of the Revolution, then of the Empire, David (1748-1825) clung fanatically to the neo-classical principles which Constable eluded and Goya surmounted. In his youth he received much the same training as his friend Madame Vigée-Lebrun (1755-1842), who painted over twenty portraits of Marie Antoinette and her children in the last years of the French monarchy. She successfully combined the styles of Greuze and Rubens (minus the latter's sensuality), together with an added feminine touch. Having traveled all over Europe, from London to St. Petersburg, painting royalty and most of the celebrities of the day, including Lord Byron and Lady Hamilton, she retired to her town house in Paris, wrote her memoirs, and died at the age of eighty-seven.

In 1784 Madame Vigée-Lebrun painted a portrait of the Comte de Vaudreuil, a typical aristocrat of the Ancien Régime, and also signed her charming, hitherto unpublished study of a "Lady folding a Letter" (Private Collection), in which the curving sheet of paper between the slender fingers is so well attuned to the sweep of the plumed hat and the light cascade of curls and silk. That same year, reacting against this demure and sentimental femininity, David produced his dramatic, not to say theatrical "Oath of the Horatii" (Louvre, Paris), with its pugnacious display of bare swords, thus inaugurating the new age of manly virtues and stern republicanism.

David himself, following the academic theory of his time, regarded historical painting as the noblest form of art. But for us it is his portraits, brushed freely and rapidly in uninhibited moments, which show him at his best, as a magnificent technician and an acute and delighted observer of people. His "Portrait of Alexandre Lenoir" (Louvre) was begun in Paris about 1815 and finished in exile at Brussels in 1817. Himself a painter, Lenoir (1761-1839) is best known as the founder and curator of the Musée des Monuments Français in Paris (still in existence today), which has been described as "the first real museum of medieval antiquities ever brought together" (Francis Henry Taylor). He was a close friend of David's and left some interesting reminiscences of the artist.

Shown in what is obviously a characteristic pose, seated at a small round table, firmly gripping the arm of his chair with his left hand, and wearing his medals and decorations, Lenoir turns slightly to one side, looking up and shifting his position in the chair as he pauses a moment for thought, with his goose quill poised over the paper. He is writing an answer to the letter whose envelope, lying beside the inkwell, is plainly addressed to "Monsieur Lenoir, Conservateur du Musée des Monuments Français."

Camille Corot (1796-1875). The Letter. (21½ × 14½″) Courtesy of The Metropolitan Museum of Art, New York.
Gift of Horace Havemeyer, 1929. The H. O. Havemeyer Collection.

One of the finest female portraits of David's heretical disciple Ingres (1780-1867) is that of the Comtesse d'Haussonville (1845, Frick Collection, New York), portrayed in her drawing room gracefully leaning against the mantelpiece on which, beside a potted plant and a pair of opera glasses, lie some letters she has just received.

Thanks to the childlike simplicity of his character and the absolute integrity of his work, Corot (1796-1875) miraculously cut across all the conflicting trends of the century with the same detachment and contemplative fervor that were shown in their own day by Vermeer and Chardin, to whom in fact, both by the technique and the spirit of his art, he was closely akin. Given belated recognition in his lifetime, and then only as a landscape painter, Corot in his last years, when old age had curtailed his rambles in the countryside, quietly accumulated in his studio a whole group of figure paintings which showed his genius in an unexpected light and came after his death as a startling revelation.

These are not so much straightforward portraits from the life, of the kind he had so diligently painted in his youth, as freely interpreted images of womanhood, symbols of the arts or embodiments of a nameless reverie, grafted to the traditional themes of reading, music-making or painting. The idea for these pictures may have come to him during a trip to Holland in the summer of 1854, where he haunted the museums and communed with Rembrandt and the Dutch intimists; both had a predilection for these subjects, and Corot's interpretations of them recapture the latter's placid serenity and the former's mysterious spirituality.

Among the series of Women Reading out of doors or in the studio, intently or abstractedly, the only one bearing on the subject of this volume is "The Letter" (Metropolitan Museum of Art, New York). The figure of the young woman, with the indolent grace of her pose and the dreamy languor of her expression, recalls those of the two masterpieces of 1865-1870, "The Studio" (Louvre, Paris) and "Interrupted Reading" (Art Institute of Chicago). Like these figures, one with a book, the other with a mandolin, this young woman is daydreaming and, wrapped in her thoughts, has left off reading the letter in her hand, which has slipped down into her lap. The muffled harmony of firmly shaded grays, browns and greens, punctuated by the reddish gleams of the hair, the glow of the pearl, and the glossy surface of the paper, together with the strength and suppleness of the brushwork, founded, as in his best Italian landscapes, on sheer structural energy and contrasting values—all this conspires to imbue this pensive figure with monumental majesty and lyrical introspection.

Corot and Courbet significantly shaped the course of things to come, but it is with Manet (1832-1883) that modern painting really begins, delivered from anecdote and academic conventions, recast in a fresh mold and embodying its own justification and autonomy. "He was the first," as Matisse put it, "to react directly to what he saw and thereby to simplify the painter's craft, expressing only what impinged directly on his senses." With him there was no intermediate step from eye to hand, from sensation to transcription, nothing picturesque or sentimental was allowed to interfere. Manet himself declared: "There's only one way for a painter to be truthful, and that is to put down straight off what he sees."

This boldness and rapidity of execution, attuned to the new rhythms of contemporary life and seconded by a masterly technique, quite bewildered a public whose tastes were still warped by official conventions, and unleashed the most violent uproar ever recorded in the annals of art history. After the storm of abuse and ridicule raised by "Olympia," his most representative

Edouard Manet (1832-1883). Portrait of Emile Zola (detail), 1868. Louvre, Paris.

work, a young art critic and novelist named Emile Zola, who was then writing enthusiastic letters from Paris to his friend Paul Cézanne at Aix-en-Provence, courageously defended the artist in April and May 1866, almost the only critic of the day to do so, and predicted that his pictures would one day hang in the Louvre. In token of his gratitude, Manet executed his portrait, begun in November 1866, finished in June 1867, and dated 1868, the year in which it was exhibited at the Salon. Both this portrait and

Achille Devéria (1800-1857). The Letter Writer, about 1830-1835. Colored chalks. (11½×9″)
Courtesy of The Cooper Union Museum, New York.

Moritz von Schwind (1804-1871). The Visit, about 1860. Watercolor. (10⅜ × 6¾″) Kupferstichkabinett, Basel.

"Olympia," as Zola foresaw, are now in the Louvre. The writer is shown in profile, seated with ease and assurance beside a rather untidy writing desk of which we illustrate an admirable detail: the inkwell with a quill pen, paper and paperknife, a pipe in a small lacquered bowl, old leather-bound volumes and others with paper covers, conspicuous among them being a series of Zola's articles on Manet reprinted in pamphlet form.

In 1872 Paul Durand-Ruel, the dealer who so courageously and selflessly supported the Impressionists when they were still unknown, suddenly bought up all the canvases in Manet's studio, some thirty pictures, for which he paid 51,000 francs. After this windfall, Manet took a new studio in the Rue de Saint-Pétersbourg, and there, from July to September 1872, he painted his favorite model, Berthe Morisot, in four different poses: with a veil, with pink shoes, with a fan, and with a bunch of violets. Then, taking these last two accessories, he composed one of his most beautiful still lifes and presented it to the young lady (whose descendants still have it today): the red fan, folded up, lies slantwise across the table, half hidden by the bunch of violets, while beside them, on the right, is a brief letter clearly addressed "A Mlle Berthe" and signed "E. Manet."

In 1879 Manet felt the first inroads of the illness that was to prove fatal four years later. In the summer of 1880 he rented a villa with a large garden at Bellevue, just outside Paris, and there took a three months' rest cure. To while away the time, he wrote almost daily letters to his friends, freely decorated with small watercolor sketches of flowers, fruit, plants, animals, profiles and any charming trifle that came to mind on the spur of the moment, all handled with a grace and liveliness no painter of his time could match. The bulk of these letters, and the most exquisite among them, were addressed to Isabelle Lemonnier, sister-in-law of the publisher Georges Charpentier.

Auguste Renoir (1841-1919). Graziella, about 1910. Detroit Institute of Arts.

Manet had just painted seven successive portraits of her in the space of a few months, and her beauty and charm were still fresh in his mind; in fact he was very much smitten with her. These short, illustrated letters have their counterpart in the occasional verses, usually quatrains, that his friend Mallarmé was writing about the same time, in very much the same spirit, and sending in many cases to the same recipients; one set of these verses bears the title "Les Loisirs de la Poste."

Manet having set the example, Cézanne, Gauguin, Van Gogh and many twentieth century artists, notably Picasso, took to illustrating their letters to their friends with pen drawings or sketches, sometimes even jotting down the initial idea for one of their major paintings.

Delacroix (1798-1863) and Courbet (1819-1877), the one inspired by the hectic visions of his imagination, the other by the epic grandeur of reality, showed little interest in intimist painting. Genre pictures and scenes of everyday life became the special province of illustrators and little masters who, quick to follow the fashion of the day, devised endless variations on epistolary themes. It would be idle to enumerate all the anecdotal and sentimental interpretations given by several generations of Rococo, Neo-Classical and Romantic artists like Henry Fuseli (1741-1825), François Gérard (1770-1837), Louis-Léopold Boilly (1761-1845), François-Marius Granet (1775-1849), Francis Danby (1793-1861) and J. A. Franquelin (1798-1839). Two particularly charming examples, one by a Frenchman, one by a German, will suffice to show the persistence of the theme and its gradual renewal in the course of the nineteenth century.

Achille Devéria (1800-1857), whose Paris studio in the Rue de l'Ouest was one of the rallying centers of the French Romantics, was a gifted, versatile and erratic artist whose career at first promised to be a brilliant one.

Though equally adept at historical paintings on academic lines and small erotic pictures in the boudoir tradition of the eighteenth century, he owed his success chiefly to his graphic work, in particular his famous gallery of lithograph portraits. Even better than his small, daintily handled picture in the Louvre, "The Letter" (formerly in the collection of King Louis Philippe), the drawing in colored chalks entitled "The Letter Writer" (about 1830-1835, Cooper Union Museum, New York) displays the finesse of his gracefully polished style at its best. Ten years later, after a brief taste of glory, he had fallen into oblivion.

Baudelaire, in his review of the 1845 Salon, tactfully did justice to Devéria's work. "All his drawings were full of charm and distinction, they breathed an indefinable mood of happy reverie. All his coquettish and sweetly sensual women were idealizations of those one saw and admired in the evening, at the concerts, at the opera, in the drawing rooms. These lithographs, which dealers buy for three sous and sell for a franc, are faithful representations of the fashionable, fragrant life of the Restoration period, over which hovered like a guardian angel the blond romantic ghost of the Duchesse de Berry."

A friend of Schubert's (whose songs he illustrated) and an exact contemporary of the poet Mörike, Moritz von Schwind (1804-1871) was born and bred in Vienna, but spent most of his life in Munich. He thus formed the link between the two artistic capitals of the German-speaking lands where, in an atmosphere of convivial jollity not unmingled with wistful melancholy, there lingered something of the chivalrous and romantic enchantments of medieval Germany. Schwind expended much of his energies on vast fresco cycles on historical and literary themes, in which, unfortunately, both his inspiration and his sense of color all too often failed him. And though he made some appealingly fresh and inventive illustrations for Goethe, "Robinson Crusoe," folk tales and ballads of the past, he was at his best in the familiar glimpses, frank and unsophisticated, which he occasionally gives us of daily or domestic life. For his famous painting in the Schack Museum, Munich, called "The Visit" or "The House of the Artist" (about 1860), he made a preliminary design in the form of a delightful watercolor, illustrated here. In an interior in the Biedermeier style, a young lady is paying a visit to her bosom friend; the latter holds in her hand the latest letter from her fiancé, while the visitor points out on the map the faraway place he has written from.

The letter theme, taken up in the late nineteenth century by Toulouse-Lautrec (1864-1901), the Nabis, and academic painters in the Dutch tradition, like Meissonier (1815-1891), was naturally absent in the work of the Impressionist landscape painters, with the exception of Guillaumin (1841-1927), Berthe Morisot (1841-1895) and Renoir (1841-1919). All his life Renoir was fond of the theme of Women Reading. The magnificent painting of "Graziella" (Detroit Institute of Arts), with a letter in her lap, is datable to about 1910, when the artist's favorite color was a generous and radiant red, over which, here, he has superimposed thin, silky coats of delicately graded whites and grays in contrast with the black velvet of the hair. The rich, full-bodied pigments, with their glowing, transparent depths, bring to mind the matchless technique of the Venetians, of Rubens, of Fragonard; but the mood and attitude of dreamy introspection recall Vermeer and Corot. No painting could bring to a close with more charm and grandeur, rooted in simplicity, this album of letter pictures in which the best painters of three centuries and many countries weave between them, on a privileged theme, a spell of secret and suggestive "correspondences."

Edouard Manet (1832-1883). Bunch of Violets and Fan, 1872.
(8¼×10⅝″) Private Collection, Paris.

THIS BOOK WAS DESIGNED AND PRODUCED BY
ALBERT SKIRA.
TEXT AND COLORPLATES WERE PRINTED BY THE

SKIRA

COLOR STUDIOS
IMPRIMERIES RÉUNIES, LAUSANNE.
FINISHED THE THIRTIETH DAY OF NOVEMBER
NINETEEN HUNDRED AND SIXTY-ONE.

PLATES ENGRAVED BY GUEZELLE & RENOUARD,
PARIS.